How to Write a
Romance

♥

Or, How to Write *Witty Dialogue,*
Smoldering Love Scenes, and
Happily-Ever-Afters

♥ ·›·›·——➤

The Team at *Avon Books*

MORROW
GIFT

An Imprint of
WILLIAM MORROW

This Journal Belongs to:

_____

Dear Romance Writers,

Avon Books has been synonymous with romance for more than seventy-five years, so who better to guide you through your journey of romance writing than our editors! From Kathleen E. Woodiwiss's iconic *The Flame and the Flower* to Lynsay Sands's Argeneau vampires, we lead our authors through character development, plot twists, and delivering that all-important happily-ever-after (HEA) ending.

When writing romance, the possibilities for innovation are endless, and there are no hard-and-fast rules for crafting a delicious tale. Our hope for this journal is that it will serve as a companion, source of inspiration, and cheerleader as you work on your current project, no matter where you are in your process. Romance is a supportive community and we're glad to welcome you (and so are our authors, who sent words of encouragement directly to you through this journal). We're so happy to be collaborating on this project and can't wait to fall in love with your hero and heroine.

xx

Editors of Avon

Note: In some cases we have used hero/heroine and he/she for expediency only. Love is love and romance is universal. Please change the sexes, gender identities, life-forms, etc., to whatever best fits your story!

Describe your heroine's physical characteristics without having her look in a mirror.

_____

_____

_____

_____

_____

_____

_____

Write an exchange in which one character drops an object and the other picks it up. What is the object?

_____

_____

_____

_____

_____

_____

_____

_____

Make a list of five to ten
of your heroine's nonphysical
characteristics. Is she stubborn?
Is she sarcastic? Does she sing
in the shower?

1 _____
2 _____
3 _____
4 _____
5 _____
6 _____
7 _____
8 _____
9 _____
10 _____

What kind of speech pattern does your hero have? What is his trademark exclamation? Describe his voice in four exchanges.

You're meeting an online match at a coffee shop
but you've been waiting for almost thirty minutes.
A sexy stranger sits down opposite you, one who is NOT
the person you swiped right on. What happens next?

The journey of a thousand miles
begins with a single step.
The completion of a book begins
with a single page.

—Karen Ranney

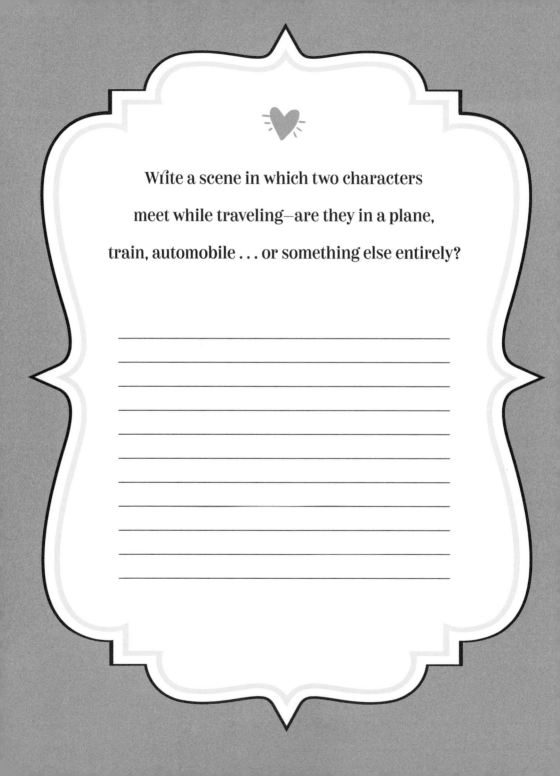

Write a scene in which two characters
meet while traveling—are they in a plane,
train, automobile . . . or something else entirely?

_____
_____
_____
_____
_____
_____
_____
_____
_____
_____
_____

How a character smells says a lot about them. List the first three scents that come to mind when thinking of your hero. (Example: he smells like leather.) Now describe your heroine using another three scents.

1 _____

2 _____

3 _____

1 _____

2 _____

3 _____

Conflict creates tension, which keeps readers turning pages. Every romance should have conflict, whether external (an outside force keeping the couple apart) or internal (emotional issues that keep a character from accepting love). The strongest stories have both! What are your novel's conflicts? Why can't your characters be together from one chapter to the next? Make some notes here.

_____

_____

_____

_____

_____

_____

_____

_____

_____

_____

_____

_____

_____

List five to ten of your hero's nonphysical characteristics—both good and bad!

1 _____

2 _____

3 _____

4 _____

5 _____

6 _____

7 _____

8 _____

9 _____

10 _____

Your heroine is wearing a fake mustache and
your hero is soaking wet. How did they end up like this?
What do they do next?

I don't know anyone who manages to write one word without first making coffee, checking email six times, reheating said coffee, emptying the dishwasher, moving the laundry from the washer to the dryer, and then checking email four more times.

—Julia Quinn

How would your hero respond to the insult

"You, sir, are no gentleman"?

Does your story have a villain?
Describe that person without commenting
on their physical appearance.

_____

_____

_____

_____

_____

_____

_____

_____

_____

_____

What hobbies do your characters have?

What do they care about outside of the relationship?

The most satisfying stories involve emotional growth
on the parts of both the hero and the heroine. How will your
characters change by the end of the story? For each, list one inner
obstacle they must overcome by the last chapter.

Scenario:

Your main character is at a rodeo and the young man
riding the bull is thrown off, landing at her feet.
What does she do next?

_____

_____

_____

_____

_____

_____

_____

_____

_____

_____

_____

_____

_____

_____

_____

_____

_____

There's only one qualification you
have to meet to be a real writer . . .
You have to sit down and write!

—Susan Elizabeth Phillips

What kind of speech pattern does your heroine have? What is her favorite curse word? Describe her voice in five adjectives.

1 _____

2 _____

3 _____

4 _____

5 _____

**What kind of relationship do your characters
have with their siblings? Is anyone an only child?
Is there bad blood between them?
Describe their emotional connection.**

_____
_____
_____
_____
_____
_____
_____
_____
_____
_____
_____
_____
_____
_____

The black moment in a romance novel is when your characters believe all hope is lost and their love will not survive. What's the black moment in your story? What conflict, fundamental difference, or emotional roadblock is standing in the way of their happiness?

_____

_____

_____

_____

_____

_____

_____

_____

_____

List five ways for your character
to reject an advance (whether they're
attracted to the person or not).

1 _____

2 _____

3 _____

4 _____

5 _____

Scenario:

Your attractive roommate is exiting the bathroom after a shower, but something startles them and the towel slips. You quickly avert your eyes but it's too late . . . you've already seen them naked. What happens next?

_____

_____

_____

_____

_____

_____

_____

_____

_____

_____

_____

_____

_____

_____

_____

Even when you're not writing you can be working on your book. Daydreaming counts. I just call that plotting.

—Sophie Jordan

It's time for your main

character to say "I'm sorry."

How do they go about it?

What is their grand gesture?

_____

_____

_____

_____

_____

_____

_____

_____

_____

Write a love scene that occurs in the bathroom
(tub or shower or countertop, you decide!).

_____

_____

_____

_____

_____

_____

_____

_____

_____

_____

_____

_____

_____

_____

_____

Very briefly outline what happens in the first five
scenes of your story. Is each situation moving the plot
and/or romance forward? Ideally, every scene should do both.
If a scene is doing neither, cut it!

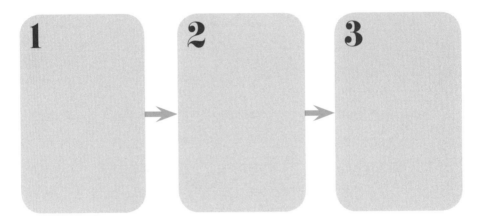

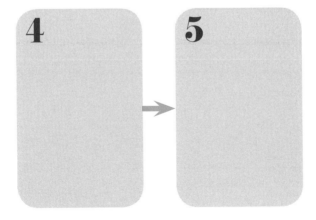

Jot down the backstory of your hero—what made him the way he is? What about him can or should change? What can't?

You're riding in a carriage through Hyde Park and a mysterious stranger jumps in. What happens next?

It takes guts to be a writer. It takes guts to be locked into a craft where you have no one but yourself to count on and no one but yourself to blame if the end product isn't what you wanted. Give yourself credit for that.

—Susan Elizabeth Phillips

Write a scene in which two female characters are having a conversation . . . that is not about a man!

Write a love scene that takes
place outdoors!

Think about your
favorite story and write
down five things that you
love about it.

1 _____

2 _____

3 _____

4 _____

5 _____

Jot down the backstory of your heroine—what made her the way she is? What about her can or should change? What can't?

Scenario:

You are an heiress and can't figure out if the
man wooing you is looking for love or looking to enrich
his coffers. So you devise a test. What is that test?

Romances love winners. There are lots of ways to be a winner; make sure you instill at least one of them in your female protagonist.

—**Charis Michaels**

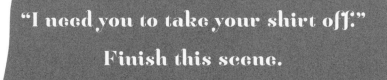

"I need you to take your shirt off."
Finish this scene.

Describe what your hero is wearing when your heroine first sees him.

_____

_____

_____

_____

_____

_____

_____

_____

_____

What is the plot of your favorite fairy tale? How would you retell it? What would you change?

Write an in-depth character bio for a villain. What makes this person evil? What are their goals, motivations? Why are they targeting your main characters? Make sure they are three-dimensional, not a caricature!

_____

_____

_____

_____

_____

_____

_____

_____

_____

_____

_____

_____

_____

_____

_____

Write a short fantasy about your favorite "shipping" couple from pop culture!

Don't try and write like someone else. Write like YOU.

—Beverly Jenkins

Write a physical fight scene.
Who is involved?
Who are they fighting? Who wins?

Describe the outfit that your
heroine is wearing the first time she
undresses for the hero.

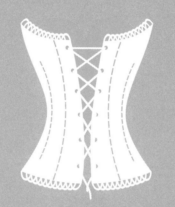

_____

_____

_____

_____

_____

_____

_____

_____

_____

What is your least favorite trope?
How would you rework it into
something you'd want to read?

"I have someone I want you to meet," her best friend said.

"Oh, but I—"

Finish this conversation.

_____

_____

_____

_____

_____

_____

_____

_____

_____

_____

Scenario:

**You're the leader of a sovereign nation and
you fall in love with a commoner—go!**

_____

_____

_____

_____

_____

_____

_____

_____

_____

_____

_____

_____

_____

_____

_____

_____

We are all entitled to success.

We are all entitled to respect.

We are all entitled to love.

—Lisa Kleypas

Write a conversation or a scene in which you show the
emotional state of a character without using the word "feel"
or "feelings." Instead, focus on the character's physiology.
(ex: "His feelings for her grew stronger." vs "His heart
pounded at the thought of waking up next to her.")

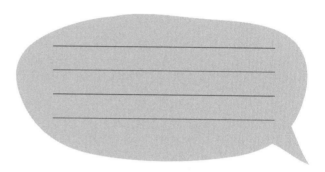

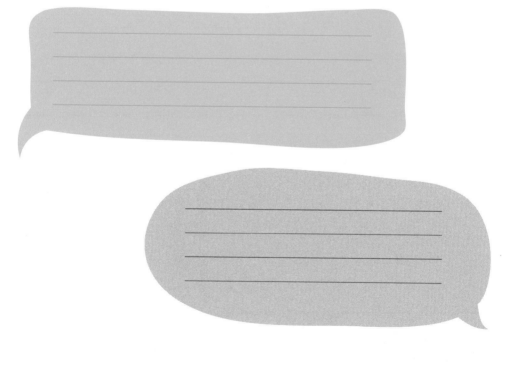

Where do your characters live
and how does it influence the story?
Do they live in a city and meet at a bar?
Do they live on a ranch and ride horses?

Briefly outline your narrative arc.
What are the beginning, middle, and end of your story?
What are the key romantic beats that advance
the story from one section to the next?

Beginning

Middle

End

Write a bio for your heroine, including her upbringing and cultural heritage. Be sure to do your research to make this character authentic!

List 5 character strengths for your heroine. Now list five character flaws.

1 _____
2 _____
3 _____
4 _____
5 _____

1 _____
2 _____
3 _____
4 _____
5 _____

If you're not sure where to go next, choose the path that makes you most nervous—the best stories are the ones told on the edge.

—Sarah MacLean

What is the first line of dialogue in your novel? Who's speaking?

," said

_____

_____

_____

_____

Your hero just woke up from a coma and has no memory of his past. Who is at his bedside? What happens next?

_____

_____

_____

_____

_____

_____

Write a scene in which your heroine sees your hero doing something that helps her better understand him and deepens her attraction.

Your character suddenly has a supernatural ability.
What is it? How is it crucial to the story?
What does it symbolize about him or her?

You're in the throes of passion when suddenly there's a knock on the door. Who is it? What happens?

_____

_____

_____

_____

_____

_____

_____

_____

_____

_____

_____

_____

_____

_____

_____

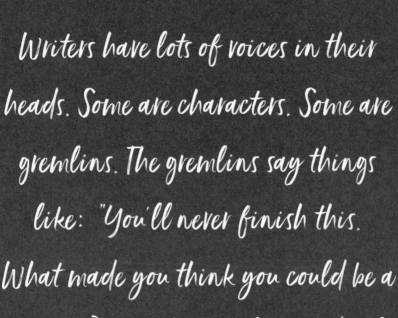

Writers have lots of voices in their heads. Some are characters. Some are gremlins. The gremlins say things like: "You'll never finish this. What made you think you could be a writer?" Drown the gremlins and only pay attention to your characters.

—Karen Ranney

Write an argument between your main couple,
including dialogue, body language, and the scene around them.
What are they fighting over?

Your heroine is secretly in love with her sibling's best friend. Describe three ways she might drop hints about her feelings.

1 _____

_____

2 _____

_____

3 _____

_____

Write a scene where your hero sees your heroine
doing something that furthers his understanding of her
and deepens his attraction.

What kind of pet would your character have?
Is it a common pet like a cat or a dog?
Is it an unusual pet like a goat or a unicorn?
What's its name? What does it eat? Describe.

Scenario:

You've moved to a new country where you don't
know the language, it's your first day, and you're lost.
Luckily, an attractive stranger successfully helps you get
to your next destination. What happens now?

You have the power and ability to reach your goals. You need passion and persistence.

—Lisa Kleypas

What does your hero say the first time he sees the heroine naked?

Write a summary of your book . . . but it cannot exceed 180 words!

_____

_____

_____

_____

_____

_____

_____

_____

_____

_____

_____

_____

_____

_____

_____

What is the worst thing that could happen to your couple?
How would they react? Would it tear them apart and become
the black moment? Or make them stronger?
Make some notes here.

List five things your characters love about each other, besides physical attributes.

1 _____

2 _____

3 _____

4 _____

5 _____

You run into your attractive new neighbor (literally) while out for a jog; they don't seem too happy, but still manage to give you the once over as you two argue about who hit whom. What happens next?

If you're stuck on a page, try living inside the scene with the character. Settle into her skin. Can she hear the heavy thud of her own heartbeat? See nothing but the flickering glow of firelight behind a mullioned window? Feel the dampness of her palm as she reaches for the doorknocker? Usually, when my senses are engaged and I'm living inside the scene, it's easier to find my way out.

—Vivienne Lorret

Describe your hero taking a bite of his favorite food.

Write a scene that shows your characters are in love . . .
without letting them touch!

What are your character's goals in this story? What are they working toward? What do they need to achieve by the end of the book? Does one character's goal directly clash with the others? Is one goal (or both) standing in the way of their HEA? Outline here.

_____

_____

_____

_____

_____

_____

_____

_____

_____

_____

_____

Do your characters have any qualities
that make them seem incompatible?
Please describe!

Scenario:

You just found out a huge secret about your partner.
When they walk in, they act as if nothing has happened
and it's clear they don't realize you know.

What do you do?

_____

_____

_____

_____

_____

_____

_____

_____

_____

_____

_____

_____

_____

_____

_____

_____

To riff on G. K. Chesterton: romance novels aren't written to show readers that love exists, they're written to show readers that they're *deserving* of it. Don't forget that as you craft your HEA.

—Alyssa Cole

Write a scene in which one character confides
in another. Why are they choosing to share this information
now? Are they hoping to gain something? Are they genuinely
in need? How is this disclosure met and what effect will it
have on the overall plot of your story?

_____

_____

_____

_____

_____

_____

_____

_____

_____

_____

_____

Write the first scene in which your characters are noticeably alone together. What is the setting? Is it intentional or an unexpected encounter?

Outline how your romantic arc will progress from climax (black moment) to resolution (reconciliation) to Happily Ever After. Is your conflict complex? Has each character realized something or learned from a mistake? Don't rush your ending!

What is your main character's profession?
Do they like their job? Why did they choose it?
Is this a career or just what they do for work?

You meant to text your best friend, but you've
accidentally sent a message to your secret crush revealing
how you feel about them. How do they respond?
What happens next?

_____

_____

_____

_____

_____

_____

_____

_____

_____

_____

_____

_____

_____

_____

_____

_____

Write the book you want to

read and can't find.

—Ilona Andrews

Write a journal entry for your heroine on
the day she first meets the hero.

_____

_____

_____

_____

_____

_____

_____

_____

_____

_____

_____

_____

_____

_____

_____

_____

Describe the look, feel, smell, and sounds of the setting where your characters first make love.

_____

_____

_____

_____

_____

_____

_____

_____

_____

Does your story have an epilogue? Outline anything that still needs to be resolved to give your readers a sense of closure after the main action of the story has finished.

Choose one of your secondary characters and describe
how they function in the story. How did they meet your
protagonist and what is their back story?

Scenario:

You run into a one-night stand while
traveling on business. Both of your flights are delayed,
so you decide to hang out and suddenly it's midnight.
What happens next?

You have to learn, and more important, you have to accept that you can't please everyone all of the time.

—Julia Quinn

Write a conflict scene between the main character and the villain.

What is your heroine's main trigger (a plot device which causes flashbacks, insightful internal dialogue, etc.)? Is it a certain smell, certain song? Be creative!

It's time to have your hero and heroine get to know each other. Describe three ways for them to interact. What activities are they doing together? What do they talk about?

_____

_____

_____

_____

_____

_____

_____

Have either of your main characters suffered a major loss? Who did they lose? How did it happen? How long ago? Does it still affect them?

_____

_____

_____

_____

_____

_____

_____

_____

You just hailed a taxi only to find a cute
but confused stranger climbing in the other door.
You both think the cab is yours and refuse to get out—
describe the ensuing ride.

_____

_____

_____

_____

_____

_____

_____

_____

_____

_____

_____

_____

_____

_____

_____

_____

_____

There is no one-size-fits-all approach to writing. Are you a plotter? Pantser? Somewhere in between? It doesn't matter! As long as your process carries you from Chapter One to The End of a book that you're proud of, you have the right process. Happy writing!

—Jeaniene Frost

A very attractive ghost
just appeared in your heroine's
living room. What does the spirit
want? List the reactions of every
character in your story.

1 _____

2 _____

3 _____

4 _____

5 _____

_____

_____

_____

_____

_____

_____

_____

_____

_____

_____

_____

_____

_____

_____

Sometimes it helps to plan the black moment of a novel first and then plot backward from there. Brainstorm an emotional, relationship-ending moment that would make for strong, complex romantic conflicts. Make some notes here.

_____

_____

_____

_____

_____

_____

_____

_____

_____

_____

_____

Imagine your character is going to see a therapist. . . . What issues
would they want to discuss? What would they be aware of and what
wouldn't they? What would the therapist say?

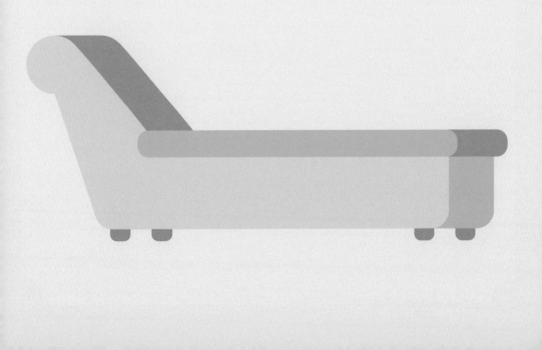

You walk into a castle uninvited and stumble
into a room where a handsome young man is working.
What is he doing? How does he react to your presence?
What happens next?

_____
_____
_____
_____
_____
_____
_____
_____
_____
_____
_____
_____
_____
_____

Never doubt that you are good
enough. Storytelling is your gift
and it should be shared.
Start writing and see where you go.

—Cathy Maxwell

Write dialogue in which your characters express their love without using the words "I love you."

Show a character's personality by describing
their wardrobe.

The big revelation is the moment

in your story when a character finally acknowledges his

or her feelings. When does this happen in your story?

What triggers this realization? Describe the scene

and outline the character's thought process.

_____

_____

_____

_____

_____

_____

_____

_____

_____

_____

_____

_____

_____

_____

_____

What would your hero's online dating profile
look like? What would his short bio say? Describe the
photo he would upload.

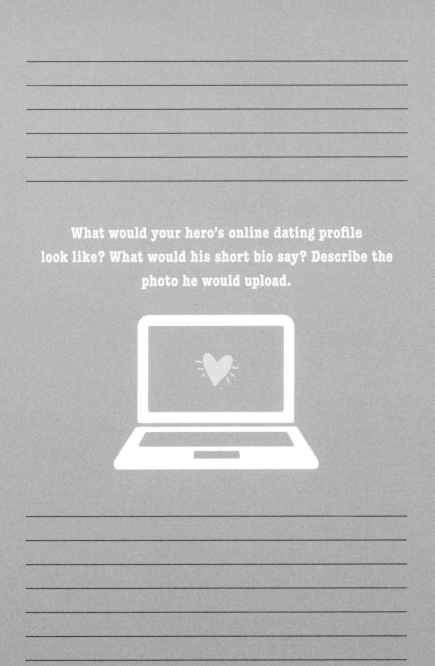

_____

_____

_____

_____

_____

_____

_____

You're a time traveler and you fall in love with
someone from the past. In what era does your lover live?
What is their social status? Do you stay in the past
or bring them with you to the future?

_____

_____

_____

_____

_____

_____

_____

_____

_____

_____

_____

_____

_____

_____

_____

_____

Make every word work for

its place in your story.

—Beverly Jenkins

What traits does your heroine reveal in a
private setting (glasses, freckles, etc.) that embarass her,
which your hero finds adorable?

Describe how the heroine responds to
physical affection from different characters:
her friends, family, the hero, the villain.

_____

_____

_____

_____

_____

_____

_____

_____

_____

_____

_____

Write a love scene in
which both characters keep most
of their clothes on.

_____

_____

_____

_____

_____

_____

_____

_____

_____

_____

_____

_____

Describe the heroine's best friend.
Is he or she three-dimensional enough
to be the next protagonist in the series?
Something worth keeping in mind!

You've just been recruited to the CIA as a spy.
On a training mission, you realize someone is tailing
you—someone with a rugged smile and confident gate.
What's your next move?

_____

_____

_____

_____

_____

_____

_____

_____

_____

_____

_____

_____

_____

_____

_____

_____

_____

Always remember the why of your love story. Why are these two characters right for each other? Knowing your why will help your readers root for your couple, and keeps them turning the pages.

—Eva Leigh

Your hero has just discovered a secret that will forever change his life. What is it? Who is the first person he tells? Write the exchange.

Describe your hero's body
and physicality: his hair tone, eye color, stature,
the way he walks.

_____

_____

_____

_____

_____

_____

_____

_____

_____

_____

_____

_____

Write a sex scene outside of the bedroom,
where your hero and heroine could be
discovered at any moment.

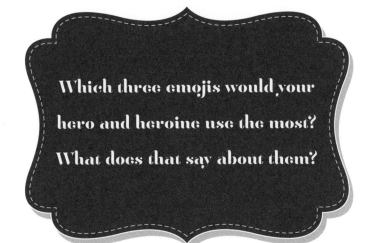

Which three emojis would your
hero and heroine use the most?
What does that say about them?

1 _____

_____

2 _____

_____

3 _____

_____

You're a sheltered lady longing for adventure.
One day, you decide to exchange clothes with your maid
so you can wander the streets of London. What's the first
thing that happens as soon as you leave your Mayfair
townhouse? Who do you encounter first?

_____

_____

_____

_____

_____

_____

_____

_____

_____

_____

_____

_____

_____

_____

_____

_____

_____

_____

Our genre supports the idea of
a women's freedom to make her
life whatever it wants to be.

—Lisa Kleypas

Write a scene in which your heroine
has to listen while another character says something
she wishes they wouldn't. How does she feel?
Why can't she speak up?

_____

_____

_____

_____

_____

_____

_____

_____

_____

_____

_____

_____

Describe a room your heroine is afraid to enter. Why is she scared to go in? Will she have to enter at one point and what will force her to?

_____

_____

_____

_____

_____

Write a love scene incorporating a chair,
a fan, and a scarf.

_____

_____

_____

_____

_____

What are some things your hero and heroine have in common? List three to five hobbies, interests, personality traits or experiences they share.

1 _____

2 _____

3 _____

4 _____

5 _____

Scenario:

As you're crossing the street to go to work,
you bump into a familiar face. Surprise! It's none
other than the person who broke your heart in school.
What's next?

_____

_____

_____

_____

_____

_____

_____

_____

_____

_____

_____

_____

_____

_____

_____

_____

Happy endings are all I can
do. I wouldn't know how to
write anything else.

—Julia Quinn

_____

_____

_____

_____

_____

_____

What is the funniest moment in your story?
Does it involve the hero and heroine, or side characters?

_____

_____

_____

_____

_____

_____

_____

_____

_____

_____

_____

_____

_____

Describe the mode of transportation most commonly used in your story. What does it say about the time period/economic status of your characters? Is it realistic to where they live (ex: if your book is set in Manhattan, would your characters really drive to work, etc.)?

_____

_____

_____

_____

_____

_____

_____

_____

_____

Write a scene that involves dancing.

Who is dancing and where?

Solo, or with a partner?

Is it sexy or classic?

What is your heroine particularly sensitive to in others?

Their judgment? Their needs?

You're a librarian and someone hands you
a book to check out: *How to Make Love All Night
(and Drive a Woman Wild)*. You look up to see who it is.
What's next?

_____

_____

_____

_____

_____

_____

_____

_____

_____

_____

_____

_____

_____

_____

_____

_____

_____

_____

_____

Ranney's Rules:
Put something on the blank page.
You can always revise later.
Never listen to the gremlins.
Feel the emotion. How can
you convey it otherwise?
Respect your characters and your readers.
Write every day.

—Karen Ranney

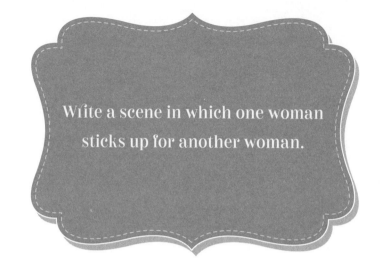

Write a scene in which one woman
sticks up for another woman.

Describe your heroine's hands. Are her nails polished or dirty? Is her skin smooth or rough, tan or pale? What does the condition of her hands say about her position in life?

Write a scene in which the hero watches the heroine dance
with another man, from his perspective.

What are your hero and heroine's political or religious
views (if any)? What do they believe in?

_____

_____

_____

_____

_____

_____

_____

_____

_____

_____

_____

_____

You buy a book you've been looking for
at a garage sale. When you go home, you see someone
has written a phone number inside, and on a whim you
decide to call it. A gravely voice picks up the other
end of the line—who is it?

_____

_____

_____

_____

_____

_____

_____

_____

_____

_____

_____

_____

_____

_____

_____

Every good romance novel is built on the irresistible force paradox: your hero and your heroine are the unstoppable force and the immovable object, and your plot is what happens when these equally powerful forces collide. If you give each character a goal, and those individual goals are in direct conflict, there's your story.

—Laura Lee Guhrke

Write a scene in which your heroine verbally dresses down your hero. Does she mean what she says or is she just angry? Is she correct and if so, does he own it?

Describe a letter written by your hero. Does he use email or a quill? What is distinctive about his writing style? What comes through in his written words that might not show when he speaks? How does he sign off?

_____

_____

_____

_____

_____

_____

**Describe the first kiss between your characters,
including the situation leading up to it and how they
react after it's over.**

_____

_____

_____

_____

_____

_____

_____

_____

_____

_____

_____

_____

_____

Does your character have an academic interest?
Did they go to college, and if so, what did they study?
What draws them to this subject?

_____

_____

_____

_____

_____

_____

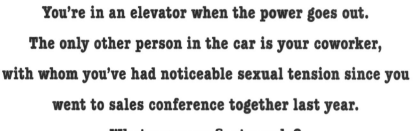

You're in an elevator when the power goes out.

The only other person in the car is your coworker,

with whom you've had noticeable sexual tension since you

went to sales conference together last year.

What are your first words?

_____

_____

_____

_____

_____

_____

_____

_____

_____

_____

_____

_____

_____

_____

_____

_____

_____

When setting up your workspace,
make absolutely sure that you cannot
reach your refrigerator without
getting up from your chair.

—Julia Quinn

Write a scene between your hero and heroine that's laden with subtext. Are there other characters in the room, and if so, whom? Can others sense the tension?

_____

_____

_____

_____

_____

_____

_____

_____

_____

_____

_____

_____

_____

Describe your heroine bathing.

What does her bathroom look like? Does she have plumbing?

Is she assisted by anyone? Servants? A sister? The hero?

Describe the heroine's ideal happily-ever-after at the beginning of the story. Is it the same as her actual happily-ever-after? If not, how so?

_____

_____

_____

_____

_____

_____

_____

_____

_____

What kind of manual skills
does your hero have? Can he build
furniture? Can he sew?

Scenario:

It's opening day at your new flower shop and who should wander in but your best friend's brother, looking to purchase a bouquet. You have liked him for years, but he's always seen you as his sister's plus one. Who is he buying flowers for? What kind? How does it make you feel?

_____

_____

_____

_____

_____

_____

_____

_____

_____

_____

_____

_____

_____

_____

_____

_____

What our genre says is that

women are important.

—Lisa Kleypas

Write a scene in which the hero and heroine agree
on something they previously quarreled over.

Describe the last book your hero read.
Did it teach him anything?

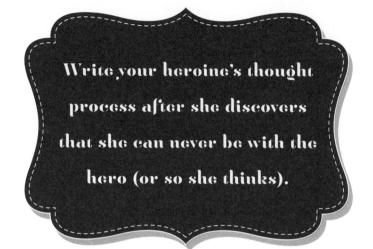

Write your heroine's thought process after she discovers that she can never be with the hero (or so she thinks).

_____

_____

_____

_____

_____

_____

_____

_____

_____

_____

_____

_____

_____

_____

_____

_____

What kind of puzzle would your heroine be best at solving?
And your hero?

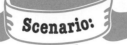

After a massive fight with your boss,

you take your pickup truck out to an old water tower to clear

your head. Only—you find someone else is already in your

spot, with problems that make yours look cute by comparison.

Who is it and what has happened?

Write what you love, and love
what you write. You are your first
audience, and if you don't love
it, why should anyone else?

—Caroline Linden

Where is your book set? What are the sights, sounds, and smells? Where does your heroine go to feel safe? Where does your hero hang out with his friends?

_____

_____

_____

_____

_____

_____

_____

_____

Describe how your heroine came to
live in her current dwelling. Is it a family home
or did she move there? What was the history of
the building before she took up residence?

_____

_____

_____

_____

_____

_____

_____

_____

Write about a social event where your characters
are surprised by one another's presence.
Who is more composed and why?

_____

_____

_____

_____

_____

_____

What is your heroine's favorite restaurant? Why?
Is there a story behind it?

_____

_____

_____

_____

_____

You are a witch who will lose her powers if she
falls in love with a mortal. After 300 years, you meet the
most handsome, kind doctor you've ever known.

What happens next?

_____

_____

_____

_____

_____

_____

_____

_____

_____

_____

_____

_____

_____

_____

_____

Don't let someone else's success make you feel less. They're on their journey. You're on yours.

—Beverly Jenkins

Write a scene in which someone attractive and charming (other than the hero) starts chatting up the heroine. How does it make her feel? How does it affect how she sees the hero by comparison?

A snowstorm has trapped your heroine in a remote
cabin with her best friend, whom she's always had a crush on.
What happens next?

List three things your character hates to do. Now describe how your character would do them. How does it make them feel?

1 _____

_____

2 _____

_____

3 _____

_____

What's the hardest thing about your hero
for your heroine to understand?
What prevents her from understanding it?

You're a firefighter who just rescued a kitten from a tree. As you hand the pet back to its six-year-old owner, someone comes running up to you. Who is it? What happens next?

Your process is your process. Figuring out what fuels us creatively, as well as what strips the juice from our writing, is part of the journey we're all traveling.

—Susan Elizabeth Phillips

Write a scene in which your heroine is
humiliated in front of your hero. What does it say
about her character that this particular event causes her
embarrassment? How does it affect his view of her?

_____

_____

_____

_____

_____

_____

_____

_____

_____

_____

Your hero is about to meet your
heroine's parent(s) for the first time.
Write the moments before their arrival.

_____

_____

_____

_____

_____

_____

_____

_____

_____

What is the biggest secret in your story?
Who would it impact the most? When is it revealed?

Your heroine is packing up her childhood bedroom
because her parents have decided to sell the family home.
What does she keep? What does she put in the donation box?
What does she throw into the trash pile?

You're a professor who has made a career studying ancient Egypt. When the opportunity arises to go study the tomb of Queen Nefertiti, you jump at the chance— and so does your infuriatingly brilliant and sexy rival, who's up for the same tenure position.
Describe the plane ride over.

_____

_____

_____

_____

_____

_____

_____

_____

_____

_____

_____

_____

_____

_____

Pour everything you have into whatever book you're writing at that moment. Don't save anything for the swim back.

—Alisha Rai

What is your hero's worst fear?

How would he react if this happened?

Write the scene.

Describe the heroine seeing an engagement ring. What is her reaction to it? Does she want one or not care? Is it a diamond or something else? Is she going to say yes or no?

Which character realizes they have fallen for the other one first? What is the precise moment they know and what triggers the realization? Write the scene.

_____
_____
_____
_____
_____
_____
_____
_____
_____
_____
_____
_____
_____
_____
_____
_____

Why does your heroine want or not want to fall in love? Does she have emotional scars from past relationships? What void in her life does she think love will fill?

_____

_____

_____

_____

_____

_____

_____

_____

_____

_____

_____

_____

_____

_____

_____

_____

You design wedding dresses for a living—
always the bridal couturier, never the bride. Then one day
the perfect man walks into the store to help his sister try
on some gowns. Describe the fitting.

_____

_____

_____

_____

_____

_____

_____

_____

_____

_____

_____

_____

_____

_____

_____

_____

Some people won't love your writing, and that's okay. It may be a difficult concept to accept, but it's true; no writer can satisfy every reader. So write from the heart and focus on telling the story you were made to tell.

—Mia Sosa

Our hero finds a pregnancy test in the trash and it reads "positive."
What happens next?

Your hero is inside an abandoned building.

Describe the setting. Who is he meeting and why?

What role does money play in your story?
How does it impact your characters? Is it a subject that
causes conflict, and if so, how?

Your heroine sees an advertisement
in the local newspaper for something that
excites her so much she drops what she's doing
immediately to inquire. Write the ad.

_____

_____

_____

_____

_____

_____

_____

_____

_____

_____

_____

Your heroine has just been named CEO of a company.
She's helming her first meeting when she spots her rival
who was also up for the job. Describe the meeting.

Find a way to get them together and keep them together. Whether it's cabin-in-the-woods, coworkers, next-door neighbors, or they're on opposite sides of a cause. Build a crucible and put your hero and heroine in it.

—Lori Wilde

Your heroine just rushed into the emergency room.
Why is she there?

_____

_____

_____

_____

_____

_____

What is your hero's most prized possession?
Where did it come from?

_____

_____

_____

_____

_____

_____

Your characters are in danger and on the run.
They're hiding out for the night in a hotel room but there's
only one bed! Write a steamy scene. Does someone
need help cleaning their wounds?

What is your hero's most treasured memory?

What about your heroine's?

The last sentence of a book is just
as important as the first. What is the
last sentence of your romance?

_____

_____

_____

_____

_____

_____

_____

_____

_____

_____

_____

_____

_____

_____

Finish the book. The world is full of first chapters.

—Julia Quinn

Notes

Notes

Notes

Notes

Notes

Notes